610.69
McA

McAlpine, Margaret.
Working in health care

06 - 71

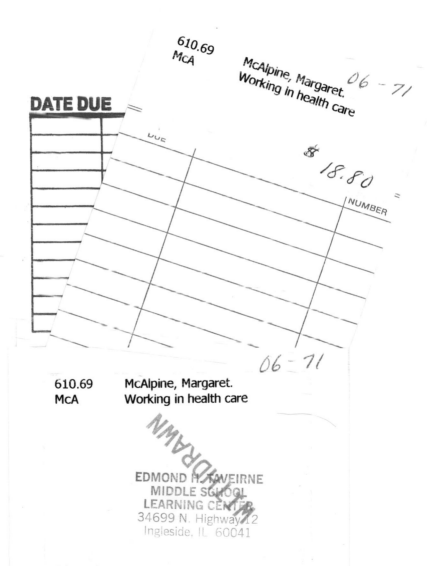

DATE DUE

$ 18.80

NUMBER

06 - 71

610.69   McAlpine, Margaret.
McA   Working in health care

My
FUTURE
CAREER

Working in

Health Care

Margaret McAlpine

GARETH**STEVENS**
GS
PUBLISHING
A World Almanac Education Group Company

P.T.O.

$18.80

06-71

Please visit our web site at: **www.garethstevens.com**
For a free color catalog describing Gareth Stevens Publishing's
list of high-quality books and multimedia programs, call
1-800-542-2595 (USA) or 1-800-387-3178 (Canada).
Gareth Stevens Publishing's fax: (414) 332-3567.

Library of Congress Cataloging-in-Publication Data

McAlpine, Margaret.
    Working in health care / Margaret McAlpine.
       p. cm. — (My future career)
    Includes bibliographical references and index.
    ISBN 0-8368-4238-3 (lib. bdg.)
      1. Medicine—Vocational guidance—Juvenile literature. I. Title.
  R690.M3527   2004
  610.69—dc22   2004045225

This edition first published in 2005 by
Gareth Stevens Publishing
A World Almanac Education Group Company
330 West Olive Street, Suite 100
Milwaukee, Wisconsin 53212 USA

This U.S. edition copyright © 2005 by Gareth Stevens, Inc. Original
edition copyright © 2004 by Hodder Wayland. First published in 2004
by Hodder Wayland, an imprint of Hodder Children's Books.

Editor: Dorothy L. Gibbs
Inside design: Peta Morey
Cover design: Melissa Valuch

Picture Credits
Corbis: Peter Beck 11, Ed Bock 9, 43(b); Bernardo Bucci 19(r); Ralph A. Clevenger
6; Corbis 15; Randy Faris 49; Jon Feingersh 24, 35(t), 48; Chris Gupton 51(b); John
Henley 46; Michael Heron 22, 23, 30; R. W. Jones 43(t); Jose Luis Pelaez, Inc. 13, 16,
17, 21, 33, 36, 41, 53, 55, 57, 59; Michael Keller 47, 51(t); Helen King 32; Gary D.
Landsman 20; Lester Lefkowitz 31, 54; Tom and Dee Ann McCarthy 38, 40, 58; Bill
Miles 44; John-Marshell Morgan 45; Warren Morgan 35(b); Roy Morsch 52; Steve
Prezant 27; Norbert Schaefer 5, 28; Tom Stewart 4, 7, 10, 29, 37, 39, 56; Strauss/
Curtis 14; James A. Sugar 8; Stephen Welstead 19(l); Ed Wheeler 25; David Woods
12, 26. **Getty Images:** cover

Gareth Stevens Publishing thanks the following individuals and organizations
for their professional assistance: Cathy Arney, LCSW, LMFT; Karen Barger, RN;
Dr. Paul Cotey, DDS; Eileen Early, RN; Mary Laan, PA; Emmylou M. Swartz,
O.D.; Ted Tousman, pharmacist.

Printed in China

1 2 3 4 5 6 7 8 9 08 07 06 05 04

Contents

Words that appear in the text in **bold**
type are defined in the glossary.

Dentist

What is a dentist?

Dentists take care of people's teeth, gums, and mouths and teach patients how to clean their teeth and keep their teeth and gums strong and healthy. People who clean and floss their teeth properly are less likely to develop cavities, gum diseases, and other problems.

Dentists also take care of dental injuries, such as chipped or broken teeth, and treat the effects that illnesses sometimes have on the condition of a person's teeth. Regular checkups help dentists detect tooth, gum, and mouth problems early so they can be cured, or at least prevented from getting any worse.

Dental specialists called orthodontists correct the position of teeth in the mouth to improve both health and appearance.

Some dentists work in clinics or hospitals, but most are self-employed and have **private practices** with dental assistants and **hygienists** to help them.

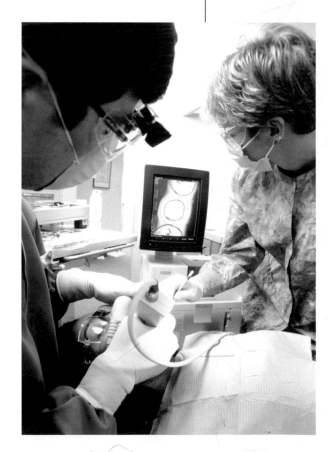

Dentists and dental assistants and hygienists often work as a team.

Ancient Teeth

Human beings have suffered as a result of tooth pain for a very long time. The remains of ancient Egyptians have been found with holes drilled in their teeth. This treatment was probably done to relieve the pain of abscesses, which are cavities that are filled with pus.

A dental assistant's job includes:

- setting out the equipment needed to treat a patient
- **sterilizing** instruments
- writing down any comments the dentist makes while checking a patient's mouth and teeth
- preparing material for fillings

A dental hygienist's job includes:

- physically preparing a patient for dental work
- cleaning a patient's teeth by **scaling** and flossing them to remove tartar, plaque, and stains
- polishing teeth to make sure they are as white and sparkling as possible
- giving advice to patients about caring for teeth and keeping them in good condition

Eating fewer sweet, sugary foods helps keep teeth healthy.

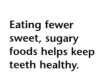

Main responsibilities of a dentist

Dentists are responsible for the health of patients' teeth and gums and provide patients with regular checkups so they can look for signs of decay or disease.

Keeping teeth healthy requires thorough cleaning. Some dentists clean and polish patients' teeth themselves, but, often, cleaning is done by a dental hygienist.

Even teeth that are well cared for can become decayed. To treat a decayed tooth, a dentist will remove the bad part of the tooth and put a filling into the cavity, or hole. When the root of a tooth becomes infected, dentists can remove it, using special instruments.

To repair a tooth that is damaged or broken, a dentist will file down the tooth and fit a false tooth, called a **crown**, over the real tooth. When teeth are too badly damaged to repair, dentists pull them out, then take measurements to have replacement teeth made.

A few months or years spent wearing braces can result in a lifetime of straight teeth.

Good Points and Bad Points

"It's very satisfying to see a patient leave with a dental problem solved and tooth pain relieved."

"During treatments, I do my best to help my patients relax and experience as little pain as possible, but my job can be very difficult when patients are extremely afraid of having treatments."

Patients usually have to wear **dentures** when all of the teeth in either their upper or lower gums have to be replaced. Dentures are false teeth attached to a plate that fits inside the mouth. When only a few teeth have to be replaced, a row of false teeth, called a bridge, is fastened between healthy teeth. Dentures and bridges are made by dental **laboratories**, but dentists have to make sure that they fit patients comfortably.

To see exactly what is going on beneath the surface of a patient's teeth and gums, a dentist takes **X rays** of the patient's mouth. When filling cavities or performing other dental procedures, dentists often give their patients local **anesthetics** to make sure they do not feel pain during their treatments.

A dental checkup starts with an examination of the patient's mouth and teeth.

Dentists who **specialize** in straightening uneven or crooked teeth are called orthodontists. They attach wires, called braces, to the teeth, and over time, slowly adjust the braces to pull the teeth into the correct positions.

Some dentists work in hospitals and perform surgeries. Conditions that often require surgery include:

- correcting a cleft palate, which is a hole in the roof of the mouth
- rebuilding a patient's mouth after damage caused by an injury, an operation, or an illness

Other dentists are involved in dental research.

Main qualifications of a dentist

Scientific knowledge

Dentists must have a high level of scientific knowledge, especially about how the human body works and how to treat teeth.

A steady hand

Because dentists work with sharp instruments, their hand movements need to be steady and very accurate. A wrong move can injure a patient or cause pain.

A strong stomach

A dentist cannot afford to be squeamish. All dentists have to deal with a certain amount of mess, including saliva and blood, as well as decayed teeth.

A great deal of learning must be done before a student qualifies as a dentist.

Dentists try to
encourage good
dental habits in
many ways.

Patience

Helping a nervous patient
relax can take a long time.
Dentists must be prepared
to move slowly, carefully
explaining what will happen
during a treatment and
answering all of the patient's
questions. Dentists who try
to hurry usually just frighten
or upset patients, making
treatments more difficult.

Friendliness

Dentists need to be warm and
sympathetic and able to put
patients at ease.

Business skills

Many dentists are self-employed. To run their businesses,
they must be organized and able keep clear and accurate
patient records and financial accounts.

fact file

Becoming a dentist requires at
least five years of college. First,
students have to study biology,
chemistry, and physics. Then,
they have to learn all about the
human body and how it works.
They also need to learn and
practice dentistry skills, such
as examining teeth and gums,
filling cavities, pulling out teeth,
and adjusting braces.

A day in the life of a dentist

Andrew Brown

Andrew qualified as a dentist six years ago. He and three other dentists work together as partners, sharing dental assistants and hygienists, as well as office receptionists.

9:30 a.m. A family comes in for their checkups. The two children have had regular checkups since they were very small, and their teeth are well cared for. I examine everybody's teeth, then give the mother's teeth a thorough cleaning.

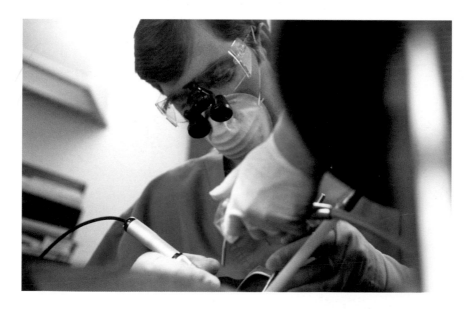

A dentist must work very carefully and accurately with any electrical equipment.

10:15 a.m. My second patient is more difficult. He stopped going to a dentist when he left college. Now, five or six years later, he has quite a lot of work to be done. I'm seeing him every two or three weeks for treatments.

11:15 a.m.   Time for a cup of coffee.

11:30 a.m.   I look at some X rays before my next patient arrives. She is twelve years old and is having some trouble biting and chewing. When she arrives, we look at the X rays together, and I tell her that I would like her to see an orthodontist.

12:30 p.m.   I update patient records on my computer.

1:30 p.m.   I eat lunch and read a dental journal to keep up with new developments.

2:30 p.m.   I take an emergency appointment. The patient is nine years old and has fallen off a wall. I clean his mouth and check to see how badly his teeth are damaged. He's frightened and upset so calming him down is not easy.

4:30 p.m.   My partners and I have a meeting to discuss a possible move to a larger group of offices. This move would also mean employing more staff.

An X ray can show a dentist a lot about the health of a person's teeth.

Doctor

What is a doctor?

Doctors diagnose, or identify, illnesses and diseases and repair injuries. They decide on the best treatments for patients and follow the progress of treatments to make sure they are successful. In some cases, doctors treat the patients themselves. In other cases, they send the patients to specialists, who are doctors with advanced knowledge about particular areas of medicine.

An important part of a doctor's work is keeping patients healthy. Doctors provide regular checkups for healthy people and give them advice on how to stay fit and well. The type of advice a doctor might give at a checkup could involve any of the following:

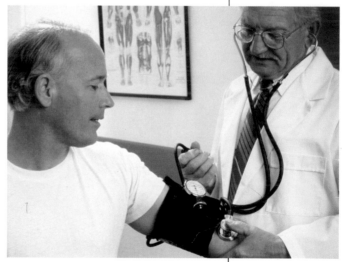

Regular health checkups are an important part of keeping well.

- eating a healthy diet
- losing weight
- exercising properly
- giving up smoking
- preventing heart disease
- getting enough sleep
- protecting skin from sunburn

Barber-Surgeons

During the Middle Ages, people who needed surgery would go to a barber-**surgeon**. Unlike doctors, however, barber-surgeons usually had no medical training at all. They performed operations using the same razors with which they cut hair and shaved beards. They also pulled out teeth and set broken bones.

Barber-surgeons attracted customers by putting red-and-white striped poles outside their shops. The red and white stripes stood for blood and bandages. These candy-cane-like poles, now commonly referred to as barber poles, can still be found outside some barber shops today.

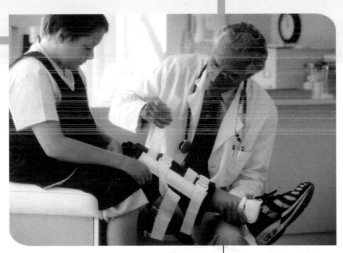

Many doctors work in the community and see patients, by appointment, in either private offices or health centers. Doctors who work mainly in clinics and hospitals often **specialize** in a particular field of medicine. Some doctors are self-employed, which means they run their own businesses and have their own offices, but many doctors are employed by hospitals or medical organizations.

Some doctors specialize in treating a particular part of the body.

Main responsibilities of a doctor

The work done by different doctors varies a great deal, and more and more doctors are choosing to specialize in particular fields of medicine. There are more than sixty fields of specialization, most of which fall into the following groups:

Medical specialities
Specialists cover most of the conditions for which people must be treated at hospitals, including:

- accidents and emergencies
- cardiology (heart diseases)
- oncology (cancers)

Surgical specialities
Surgeons perform operations on different parts of the body, such as:

- the brain (neurosurgery)
- bones (orthopedic surgery)
- the heart (cardiovascular surgery)

Pediatricians are specially trained to treat infants and children up to age eighteen.

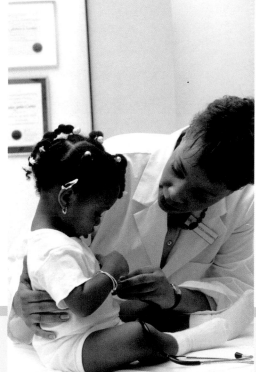

Good Points and Bad Points

"As an anesthesiologist, helping patients avoid unbearable pain gives me great satisfaction."

"Training to become a doctor means giving up your personal life."

Psychiatry

Psychiatrists work with people who are suffering from mental illnesses or **disabilities**, including **depression** and **phobias**.

Pediatrics and child health care

Pediatricians specialize in the health care of infants and children.

Obstetrics and gynecology

Obstetricians and gynecologists deal mainly with pregnancies and childbirth, but they also treat women's diseases and help women stay healthy.

Pathology

Pathologists investigate the causes and effects of diseases.

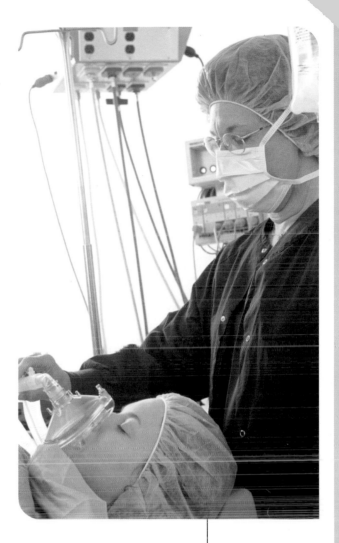

Anesthesiologists keep patients from feeling pain during surgeries.

Radiology

Radiologists produce images of the inner body with **scans** and **X rays** to help diagnose diseases and injuries and use radiation to treat cancers and other illnesses.

Anesthesiology

Anesthesiologists administer and control **anesthetics**, which are the drugs and other substances used to put patients to sleep during operations and treatments.

Medical knowledge and training

Every area of medicine has a lot to be learned. Medical studies are at a high level of academics, and a doctor's training is very long. Doctors' responsibilities, in general, from examining patients and diagnosing symptoms to doing tests and prescribing medications, take a great deal of skill, knowledge, and patience.

Commitment

Being a doctor is often made to look glamorous. Television programs, for example, often show good-looking doctors leading exciting lives, but these shows do not give a true picture of a doctor's life. Most doctors work long hours and often go home exhausted.

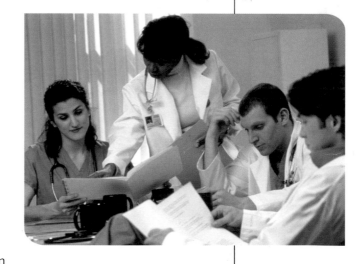

Friendliness and compassion

Doctors must be able to put their patients at ease, especially when they are worried or frightened, and comfort patients and their families in many situations. Being understanding is an essential quality for any doctor.

A medical team often includes several different doctors, as well as nurses and surgeons.

Teamwork

No doctor, not even a **general practioner**, works alone. Every doctor works as part of a team that includes nurses, pharmacists, and **therapists**. All of these professionals work together to give patients the best possible care.

fact file

Becoming a doctor takes many years of study. After four years of premedical college course work, a student must earn a medical degree and work as an **intern**, treating patients under the supervision of qualified medical staff. Once certified, a doctor must continue to study medical advancements.

A strong stomach

Doctors deal with extremely messy situations on a regular basis, including not only blood and vomit but also crushed limbs, severe burns, and badly injured tissues and organs.

Emotional strength

No matter how hard doctors try, they cannot make every patient well. They should try to take on each case with a positive attitude, but they also have to accept that some patients will not recover from their illnesses or injuries.

A day in the life of a doctor

Jane Allen

Jane works as a general practitioner associated with the **intensive care** unit of a busy hospital.

7:00 a.m.   I arrive at the hospital and go immediately to the intensive care unit (ICU) to check on a patient who was admitted through the emergency room (ER) last night. An ER doctor called me at 2:00 a.m. to ask about the patient's medical history.

7:30 a.m.   My physician's assistant arrives at the hospital. We divide my other fourteen hospital patients between us and begin rounds.

8:30 a.m.   I head back to my office.

9:00 a.m.   I'm scheduled to see eight patients this morning. One has bronchitis. Another has gastrointestinal problems. One patient, who is going through a divorce, has a sleeping disorder and thinks he is developing Alzheimer's disease. He's almost relieved to find out that his problem is depression. Another patient is pregnant. I tell her the news, then deal with her astonishment.

11:00 a.m.   I'm running behind now, so I can spend only about fifteen minutes with each patient.

12:30 p.m.   I eat a bag lunch while I dictate some notes on my morning appointments and return some phone calls from patients.

1:30 p.m.   I have to tell my first afternoon patient that her lab tests for **diabetes** came back positive. I give her dietary guidelines and instructions on how to do insulin checks and treatments.

2:00 p.m. I see seven more scheduled patients and squeeze in an emergency patient with a wide cut on his face. The cut needs a lot of stitches. I clean and bandage it, then send the patient to a plastic surgeon. In this case, a specialist can do a better job of avoiding a scar than I can.

5:00 p.m. Before I head home, I call to check on my ICU patient and finish dictating notes on all of today's patients.

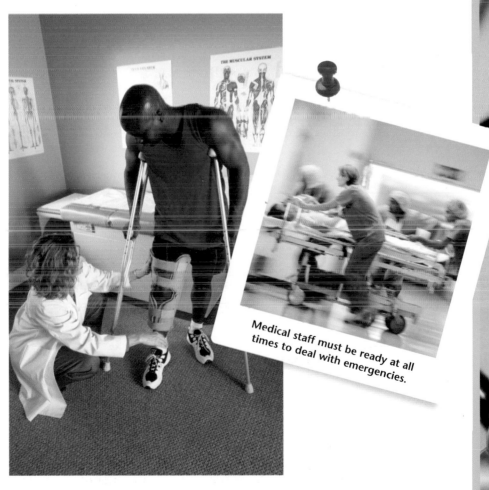

Medical staff must be ready at all times to deal with emergencies.

Some injuries need a lot of follow-up care.

Home Health Care Provider

What is a home health care provider?

Home health care providers assist patients with medical and many other kinds of care at the patients' homes. They help people who are too ill, weak, or disabled to manage their own care, but do not need hospitalization.

Nurses, physical **therapists**, **social workers**, and home health care aides are some of the professionals who provide home-based care. Becoming a home health care provider, however, requires extra education to learn how to handle patients of all ages in a variety of home situations.

Home health care providers are usually employed by **agencies** that **specialize** in taking care of people at home. These agencies carefully select the right people to provide the kind of care each patient needs, and the agencies always stay in close contact with their home health care workers to make sure everything is going well.

Home health care providers assist patients in many ways and in their own homes.

Helping Hands

Home health care providers come from many different work backgrounds. Whatever their backgrounds, however, they all must have the desire and practical skills to help people who need their special care.

While encouraging patients to be as active and involved in their own care as their health situations allow, home health care workers do whatever they can to provide both practical and medical assistance. They may have to help patients bathe, get dressed, or fix meals, or they may need to take patients for short walks. They also keep notes and records on patients' activities and progress.

Home health care providers give comfort and support as well as medical assistance.

The assistance home health care workers provide often goes beyond patient care. Patients' families sometimes need help, too. Taking care of family members who are ill or disabled is difficult. Home health aides support patients' families as a way of helping the patients get better care. They may, for example, help the family work out a system to keep track of the patient's medications.

Main responsibilities of a home health care provider

Home health care providers assist people with many health and **disability** problems, but, most importantly, they give the practical support that allows people with health needs to live at home. Without home health care, patients might have to move into nursing homes or assisted living facilities. Home care is less expensive than assisted living, and it is usually more comfortable for patients to be in their own homes, with their own furnishings, where, in many cases, they are able to enjoy the daily company of families, friends, and neighbors.

During morning visits, a home health care provider may help a patient get dressed and fix her hair.

The main responsibilities of home health care providers include the following:

- keeping a close watch on patients' health and making sure they take their medications
- assisting with routine activities, such as meals and personal **hygiene**

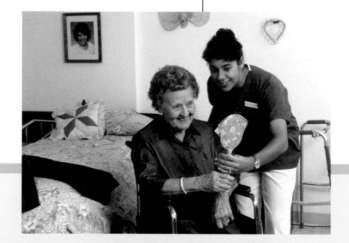

Good Points and Bad Points

"I enjoy working with patients in a family home. The atmosphere is relaxed, and it gives me a chance to talk to family caregivers about any worries they may have. I think my patients get better care from their families as a result of my visits. Sometimes, however, all the traveling I do becomes tiring, especially when the weather is bad, and I'm alone in my car."

- helping patients use safety equipment, such as walkers
- providing valuable social contact

The assistance home health care providers offer patients' families can include:

- helping with some of a patient's physical care
- providing medical and practical advice
- helping family members understand a patient's illness or disability and learn how to cope with it

Home health care providers monitor conditions that can affect the health of their patients, such as poor diets and low standards of cleanliness. Sometimes, they have to suggest different ways of doing things, including better shopping or housekeeping routines. In these situations, tact is extremely important.

Helping them prepare healthy meals has both medical and practical benefits for home care patients.

Main qualifications of a home health care provider

Special education and training
Every home health care provider, regardless of his or her professional background, must get extra education and training that provides the knowledge and skills for this special kind of patient care.

A warm, friendly personality
To help patients, home health care providers have to win their confidence and cooperation. Patients are more likely to trust people who are warm and friendly.

Patience and tact
People who are worried and unwell can often be rude or get angry easily. Home health care providers need to deal with them patiently and tactfully.

Communication skills
Under the stress of health problems, patients can easily become confused. Home health care aides need to answer questions and explain complicated situations clearly and simply.

A home health care provider must always try to be calm, friendly, and reassuring.

Understanding
Home health care providers walk into many distressing situations. They must be able to face these situations without appearing to be shocked and without judging people for things they do or how they live. A home health care worker's only job is to help.

Physical strength
Because they may need to perform physically demanding tasks, such as lifting patients, home health care workers need to be strong and physically fit.

Home health care often means encouragement for a patient on the long road to recovery.

fact file

Home health care providers are often fully trained nurses. Other people become home health care providers after getting special training and supervised experience with patients.

Organization skills

Some home health care providers are in charge of scheduling and planning their home visits themselves. To do this job well, they must be very organized and know how to make the best of their time. They may need, for example, to prepare timetables for seeing patients, and with the traveling they do, they have to know how to read maps and how to plan ahead.

Martha Brown

Martha is a nurse who works for a home health care agency.

8:00 a.m.   I call the agency to check my schedule. I have four patients to visit today.

8:30 a.m.   My first patient is an elderly man who has been unwell for about five years. His wife takes good care of him, but I visit several times a week to help her bathe him and to check his medication. I stay for a couple of hours each visit. My visits give the patient's wife time to do some shopping, spend a little time with friends and other family members, or just rest for a while. When I'm alone with the patient, he often talks to me about things that are worrying him.

10:30 a.m.   My second patient is an elderly woman who lives alone. She has had a stroke, so I have to help her shower and get dressed. I also assist her with exercises that her physical therapist has taught me to do with her.

12:30 p.m.   On this visit, the patient is a ten-year-old girl who recently had back surgery. First, I help her mother bathe her, which requires careful lifting.

Without a home health care provider, this man would have to live in a retirement home.

Home care patients are often on medications prescribed by their doctors. Home health care providers check that patients are taking their medications regularly.

Then I help the girl with some homework that a visiting teacher left for her to do. This patient likes to talk a lot about her friends at school. She should be able to go back to school in two weeks.

2:30 p.m. My last patient is a man who is ninety-six years old. His wife is ninety-four. After I bathe him, I put a special lotion on his legs to help keep his skin healthy. I often prepare meals for this couple, and I also try to clean up a little in the kitchen and the bathroom for them during my visits.

4:30 p.m. I read through my notes on all the people I've seen today, then I call the agency to tell them I have completed my visits.

Mental Health Worker

What is a mental health worker?

Mental health workers deal with patients who suffer from **anxiety**, **depression**, and a variety of other emotional and psychological difficulties.

Mental health problems affect some people throughout their lives and others only at certain times in their lives. Sometimes, people are able to work through these kinds of problems without assistance, but many people need help before they can even begin to recover.

In the past, people with mental health problems were sent to large hospitals to be treated. Often, they were kept in the hospitals so long that they became unable to manage life on their own, outside the hospital.

Part of trying to help patients with mental health problems is listening very attentively.

Opening the Door to Mental Health

Most people find talking about physical illnesses, or illnesses of the body, much easier than talking about mental illnesses, or illnesses of the mind. One in six people, nevertheless, suffers from some type of mental illness or mental disorder at some time in his or her life. This statistic means that mental health problems are as common as asthma.

Today, mental health patients are treated very differently. Although some people with mental health disorders must still be admitted to hospitals, many more continue living in their own homes and communities. Mental health workers provide many levels of support to help these patients remain independent and live their lives to the fullest. Also, a number of new medications now allow people with a variety of mental illnesses to lead almost normal lives.

Some mental health workers are based in medical centers or clinics, where they work as part of medical teams. Some run **day centers** for patients who live at home. Others work in residential facilities where groups of patients live together under the care of trained staff.

Mental health workers are also involved in drug- or alcohol-dependency programs, which help people who have problems linked to the use of these substances.

When a patient returns home after a stay in a hospital, his or her mental health worker maintains close contact to help the person settle back into normal daily life.

Main responsibilities of a mental health worker

Most mental health workers have to deal with a wide range of mental health problems. Besides anxiety and depression, these problems include **phobias**; eating disorders, such as **anorexia** or **bulimia**; and drug or alcohol abuse.

The responsibilities of mental health workers include:

- forming good relationships with patients and winning their trust and confidence
- helping patients gain the confidence they need to feel good and lead normal lives
- noticing changes in patients' behavior, which may show whether or not a patient is improving

Some patients are able to deal with certain types of mental health problems through art activities that are carefully guided by a mental health worker.

Good Points and Bad Points

"Today, many people who, at one time, might have had to spend their lives in hospitals are able to live in their own homes, make friends, and even hold down jobs. I'm proud to think that I have helped make this difference."

"Working in mental health can be exhausting, especially when a patient is not showing progress under any kind of treatment."

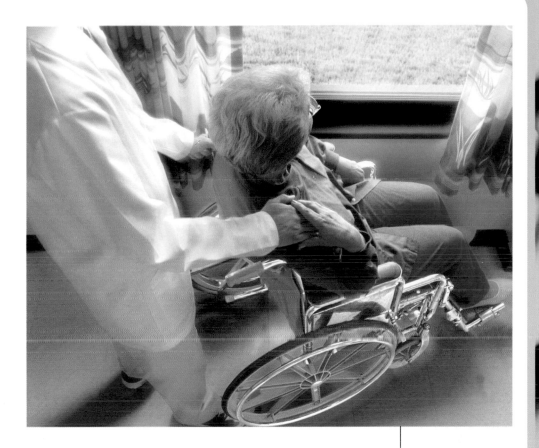

- providing different kinds of therapies or treatments, such as counseling, which involves talking over problems and their possible causes with a mental health worker, either in private sessions or in small groups, or guided activities that encourage patients to express how they feel through art, music, or drama
- monitoring patients' medications to make sure they take them in the right amounts and at the right times
- recognizing when a patient's mental problems require hospital care or some other kind of medical treatment
- helping families and friends of patients understand what is happening to the patients and how they can help, as well as how they can get over any feelings of shame that, for a long time, have been commonly associated with mental illnesses

At times, a patient may feel as if a mental health worker is his or her only source of hope and comfort.

Main qualifications of a mental health worker

Friendliness and concern
People with mental health problems are not always easy to help. They can be quiet and withdrawn, nervous or angry, and, sometimes, even violent. Mental health workers must be able to win patients' confidence before they can begin to help them.

Patience and a positive attitude
Treatments cannot be hurried so progress is often very slow. Mental health workers must, however, remain positive and keep encouraging their patients, even when treatments last for many years.

The progress of patients is often reviewed by a team of mental health professionals.

Observational skills
Restlessness, tiredness, and other symptoms can be early warnings of mental health problems. Workers must be aware of these signs, no matter how small, and start treatments before the problems become more serious.

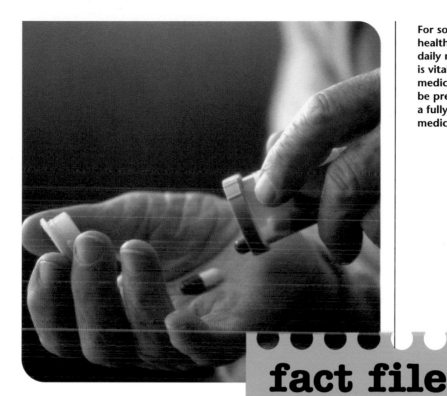

For some mental health problems, daily medication is vital, but any medication must be prescribed by a fully qualified medical doctor.

Calmness and gentleness

People with mental health problems often suffer from extreme **mood swings**. They may be content one minute and upset the next. Mental health workers need to be able to stay calm in these situations and gently help the patients calm down as well.

Teamwork

A good support system is the best way to help people with mental health problems. Working closely with **therapists, psychiatrists**, and **social workers**, a mental health worker becomes part of a team that provides support for patients.

A day in the life of a mental health worker

Frank Jeffs

Frank is one of several mental health workers associated with a medical practice in a large clinic.

8:30 a.m.   My morning starts with a team meeting, when we all get together to discuss any matters about our patients that are concerning us.

10:00 a.m.   I visit one of my patients. Although she has been in the hospital for long stretches, she now seems to be managing well at home. Her husband and daughter are there when I arrive, and we all talk about the patient's medications. I also suggest that she start coming to our day center several times a week to meet people and talk to the staff.

11:00 a.m.   I arrive at the day center and notice a young man who is very **agitated**. I take him aside and try to help him calm down. The patient tells me he is upset because he's having trouble remembering to take his medication. He also finds the company of other people upsetting. After we talk for a while, the patient agrees that I should contact his psychiatrist. Together, we will try to come up with some ideas that might help this patient.

12:30 p.m.   The psychiatrist's secretary returns my phone call to arrange a time for us to talk.

1:00 p.m.   I eat at my desk while I review phone messages and return a few calls.

1:30 p.m.   I spend some time with patients at the day center. I also observe an art therapy session and make notes on patients' behaviors and progress.

3:00 p.m. After a phone conversation with the psychiatrist treating the day center patient I saw this morning, I suggest to the patient that he start having daily visits from the community psychiatric nursing team, and he should make arrangments to see his psychiatrist after the first few visits.

4:30 p.m. I return to the medical center to write notes and reports about the day's events for my colleagues. Before going home, I check my appointments for tomorrow so I can be well prepared.

Mental health workers learn how to talk to patients in ways that will comfort and reassure them.

A mental health worker's goal is helping patients and their families enjoy life again.

Nurse

What is a nurse?

Nurses care for people who are sick, injured, or disabled. They also teach people the importance of keeping physically fit and well.

In addition to working in hospitals, nurses work in doctor's offices, clinics, health centers, rehabilitation centers (where people recover from long-term illnesses or health problems), nursing homes, the armed forces, prisons, and schools. They also work in the community, providing care for people in their own homes.

Nurses work in hospitals, nursing homes, and hospices.

The field of nursing has different specialties. Nurses can choose, for example, to work with children or with adults or in mental health nursing. Nurses who work in hospitals can **specialize** in particular areas, such as:

- oncology (caring for patients suffering from cancer)
- surgery and recovery (caring for patients during operations and immediately afterward)
- **intensive care** (caring for very sick people who need a great deal of attention)

The Lady of the Lamp

In 1854, Florence Nightingale took a group of nurses to Scutari, in Turkey. There, they looked after soldiers who had been wounded in the Crimean War. Florence used to walk around the wards at night, checking on her patients by the light of her lamp. She became known as "the Lady of the Lamp." Florence later realized that the dirty conditions in which the soldiers were nursed had caused many deaths so she introduced strict rules of cleanliness and **hygiene** to nursing.

- emergency room (caring for people with sudden and serious illnesses or injuries)

Nurses often answer medical questions as they check patients.

Emergency room staff use their assessment skills to decide whether to treat their patients in the emergency room or send them to different wards or to have surgery.

Hospital patients need to be cared for twenty-four hours a day, so nursing shifts are needed around the clock. Nurses often work at night, on weekends, and on many holidays. They have to learn to balance these unusual hours against the needs of their families and friends.

Main responsibilities of a nurse

Nurses work with many other health professionals, including doctors, **dietitians**, physical **therapists**, **x-ray** technicians, and **social workers**. Their main responsibilities are to give their patients medical care and answer their questions. They usually manage to form good connections with patients in the short amount of time they have available.

All nurses look after the sick, but there are differences between the jobs performed by nurses who work in hospitals and those who work in the community.

Hospital nurses work as part of medical teams and are typically assigned to specific wards. Their responsibilities include:

Nurses work in operating rooms with **surgeons**.

- regularly collecting and recording information about patients, which involves checking temperatures and

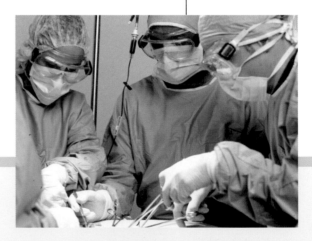

Good Points and Bad Points

"No two days are ever the same in nursing, and that's what I like about my job. The unexpected is always happening, challenging me to do my best. Often, however, the work is physically and emotionally demanding, and, although I do my best not to show it, I am always upset when, despite my efforts, patients don't get better."

pulse rates and measuring blood pressure levels
(Nurses must be able to complete precise
measurements and record them accurately.)

- cleaning and dressing wounds
- giving patients
  medications and
  injections (Nurses
  are responsible for
  making sure that
  patients receive the
  right medications
  at the right times.)
- assisting doctors
  in operating rooms,
  usually by checking
  on the health of the
  patients who are
  having surgeries or
  surgical procedures

Community nurses
provide health care
services at schools,
churches, community
centers, and social
organizations. Their
work involves:

- taking blood samples
- giving medications and
  immunizations
- screening for **diabetes**
- providing asthma treatments
- checking patients' progress
- educating people on how to
  prevent diseases

Some nurses
choose to
specialize in
caring for
premature
babies.

Main qualifications of a nurse

Knowledge of science and medical procedures
Nurses need special training to learn all about the human body and how it works. They also need to know how to care for people who are ill.

Attention to detail
Nurses must make sure that every part of their work is done exactly as it should be. Any change in a patient, even a very slight one, must be written down or reported to colleagues.

A gentle touch
When cleaning wounds, removing dressings, or taking out stitches, nurses need to work with great care so that patients experience as little pain as possible.

A friendly approach
Being ill or injured can be a frightening experience. Nurses need to help patients talk about their concerns and try to reassure them.

Before going off duty, nurses brief the new team on the progress of all patients.

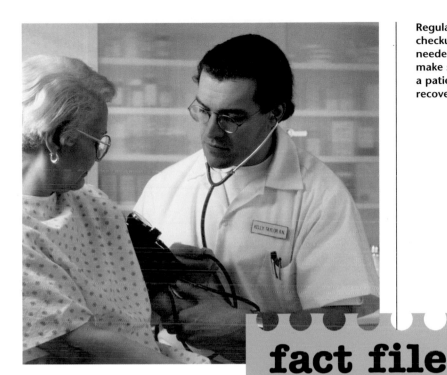

Regular checkups are needed to make sure a patient is recovering.

Communication skills
Patients want to know what is wrong with them and what treatments they will be given. Nurses have to explain things to patients clearly so they will understand what is happening.

Writing skills
Every detail of a patient's progress and treatments must be recorded on charts and in reports. This information has to be very clear to avoid any misunderstandings.

A strong stomach
Nurses have to deal with blood, vomit, and people in pain, and they must face these situations calmly.

fact file

A nurse must have either a diploma or a degree from an accredited nursing program. Nurses must also complete practical experience that is supervised by qualified health care professionals.

John Whittaker

John is a nurse on a critical care (intensive care) ward. At the moment, he is working nights, so he spends most of the day sleeping. During the week, he works two long shifts and two shorter ones. Today, he's working a long shift.

6:00 p.m. I get up and get ready for work.

9:00 p.m. Together with the rest of the night team, I'm briefed by the staff who are finishing the previous shift. All the patients on the critical care ward need a great deal of attention. The shift change is the time to listen to the day staff and ask questions. We need to be prepared for anything that might happen during the night ahead.

10:00 p.m. We check our patients, assess their **vital signs**, administer treatments, and make sure the patients are comfortable.

1:00 a.m. I check a middle-aged man who came in this morning after having a heart attack. I notice that his pulse and breathing are becoming faster. Reading the cardiac monitor, I can see, within a few seconds, that the patient has an irregular heartbeat. I call a doctor immediately and report the situation. Because I detected the irregular heartbeat, we were able to give the patient medication that will hopefully prevent him from having a second heart attack.

3:00 a.m. I take a late break.

3:30 a.m. I wonder how an elderly patient is doing and go back to the ward to check on him.

4:00 a.m. As I continue with my rounds, I also deal with a series of phone calls about transferring a patient from the emergency room.

6:00 a.m. It's getting light outside. It's time to think about the coming shift change and start writing up charts so that my reports are complete. Then I need to be available to answer questions about particular patients for workers on the next shift.

8:30 a.m. Many people are just getting up about now, but I will soon be going to bed.

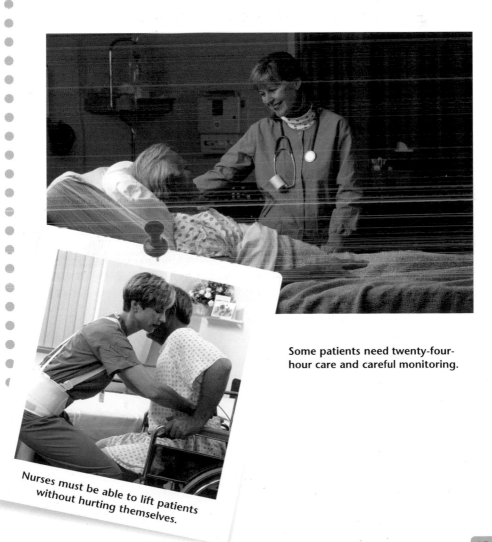

Some patients need twenty-four-hour care and careful monitoring.

Nurses must be able to lift patients without hurting themselves.

Optometrist

What is an optometrist?

Optometrists are doctors who examine people's eyes to find and treat vision problems as well as eye infections, injuries, and diseases. Not everyone has perfect vision, and even people who have good eyesight when they are young may need to wear glasses when they are older. Some children wear glasses for only a short period of time, usually to correct a condition called "lazy eye."

Some people do not realize they have sight problems until reading small print becomes very difficult.

Who Invented Glasses?

Glasses, or spectacles, have been around for hundreds of years, but no one knows exactly when they were invented or who invented them. The first glasses may have been made in Italy during the thirteenth century, but they may also have been invented in China at about the same time. At first, glasses balanced on the bridge of the nose. Bows over the ears were not added until the seventeenth century.

Today, many people wear contact lenses instead of glasses. Contact lenses are small pieces of plastic that rest directly on the eye. Laser treatments are also becoming very popular. Laser surgery corrects vision permanently and can be performed in a doctor's office, using just a local **anesthetic**.

Some people have to start wearing glasses at a young age.

After examining a patient's eyes and testing the patient's vision, an optometrist will, if necessary, prescribe glasses or contact lenses. Some optometrists order these items for their patients, too. During a follow-up appointment, the optometrist checks and adjusts the new glasses or contacts to make sure they fit properly.

Main responsibilities of an optometrist

Optometrists perform eye tests to determine the strength and type of lenses needed to correct their patients' faulty vision. Using special instruments, they also look at both the outsides and the insides of the eyes to make sure they are healthy and not injured in any way. Optometrists can treat eye injuries and prescribe medications that will heal eye infections.

Optometrists routinely check patients for eye diseases, and medical doctors often send patients to optometrists to check for eye problems caused by **diabetes**, **anemia**, and other illnesses. Optometrists refer patients to eye specialists if they suspect very serious problems, such as:

An optometrist can look inside a patient's eye using a special instrument that is called an **ophthalmoscope**.

- glaucoma, which is damage to the **optic nerve** caused by fluid pressure inside the eye
- detached retina, which is a loose inner lining at the back of the eye

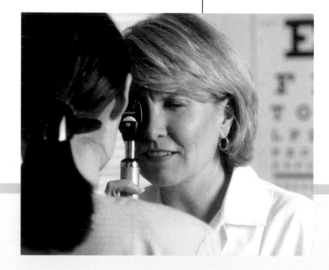

Good Points and Bad Points

"I enjoy watching children put on their first pair of glasses. Their faces just light up because they can suddenly see all the detail around them. It's as if they are seeing the world for the first time."

"The schooling to be an optometrist is very expensive. I have student loans that I will be repaying for the next twenty-five years."

- cataracts, a condition that makes the lens inside the eye dull instead of clear, causing blurred vision

Occasionally, optometrists help their patients choose frames for their glasses, which involves taking several measurements to make sure the frames fit properly. When patients prefer contact lenses, optometrists help them identify the types and brands most suitable for their eyes. Prescription eyewear can be ordered from many companies that **specialize** in manufacturing glasses or contact lenses. These days, however, eyewear is also produced locally and can sometimes be ready in as little as an hour's time. After new glasses or contacts are delivered, optometrists check the products against the original prescriptions and measurements. They also give patients advice on how to care for their eyewear.

Choosing the correct frames for a pair of glasses is very important. They should be both comfortable and attractive.

Main qualifications of an optometrist

Scientific knowledge
Optometrists need to understand and recognize eye defects and know how to correct them. They also need to know how the whole body works because some eye problems are linked to health conditions, such as high blood pressure, diabetes, or **brain tumors**.

A gentle touch
Eyes are very sensitive. Anyone who works with them needs to have a gentle touch and be extremely careful.

Communication skills
The explanations that optometrists give to patients need to be clear and simple because patients often do not understand many scientific or medical terms.

A friendly manner
A patient's job is to hold still during an eye examination and concentrate during the vision test. The optometrist's job is to put the patient at ease for all procedures.

Most people wear contact lenses to improve their vision, but some people wear them to change the color of their eyes.

Today, some frames for eyeglasses are created by famous fashion designers

Business skills

Many optometrists are self-employed, which means they need to keep accurate, detailed financial records, as well as up-to-date patient records, and make all the right decisions to keep their businesses profitable.

Ongoing education

Optometrists must constantly keep themselves informed about advancements in eye care and vision correction.

fact file

Optometrists must earn an O.D., or Doctorate of Optometry, degree, which requires a college bachelor's degree, four years of optometry school (including two years of clinical training), and passing board exams.

Lauren Burgess

Lauren is one of seven optometrists working in a large practice with modern offices located in a shopping mall.

9:00 a.m. An elderly patient who has had mild cataracts for a while complains of blurred vision. I examine her eyes and find that the cataracts have gotten worse, and she will need surgery to improve her vision. I explain the process to the patient and refer her to a local eye **surgeon**.

10:00 a.m. A fifty-three-year-old patient, who currently wears bifocal glasses, would like to try bifocal contact lenses. We discuss the pros and cons, then set up an apppointment for a contact lenses fitting.

10:30 a.m. A mother brings in her three-year-old son. She says that his right eye turns inward, especially when he is tired. Since the boy is too young to read an eye chart, I do special vision tests. I discover that he is very farsighted, and his eyes are trying so hard to focus that the right eye turns inward. I prescribe glasses and tell the boy's mother to bring him back in three months so I can check his progress.

12:00 p.m. I have lunch with a local eye surgeon. We talk about new techniques in **LASIK** eye surgery, new glaucoma medications, and the latest technology for detecting glaucoma.

1:30 p.m. A nineteen-year-old college student who wears clear contact lenses would like colored contacts to change her eye color. I fit her for colored lenses and schedule a follow-up visit to check the fit.

2:00 p.m. I still have to see four more patients. One needs contact lenses refitted, and all of them need vision tests to see if their current prescriptions need adjusting. I routinely check the health of every patient's eyes.

5:00 p.m. My last patient of the day is a forty-three-year-old man who wears glasses. He says he has to take his glasses off to read anything up close. I quickly determine that he now needs bifocals.

One part of a vision test involves reading rows of letters on a chart. In each row, moving down the chart, the size of the letters gets smaller.

These days, eyeglasses come in a wide variety of shapes and styles.

Pharmacist

What is a pharmacist?

Pharmacists are experts in the use of medicines and drugs. They make up medicines according to doctors' instructions and give them to people with information on how and when to take them. They also offer advice on pain relief and on treatments for minor **ailments**, such as indigestion, allergies, coughs, and colds.

Long ago, only herbs and other plants were used to treat illnesses and heal injuries.

Apothecaries

Early pharmacists were known as apothecaries and had little medical knowledge or training. Most of them did, however, have some understanding of **botany** and chemistry and used this knowledge to make medicines, which they sold to people to cure illnesses. Apothecaries' medicines were often made from plants and herbs they grew in their gardens. Some of the medicines were helpful. Many were of no use at all.

All pharmacies and any other places where drugs are sold must be under the direct control of a qualified and registered pharmacist. Most pharmacists work in retail stores, such as drug stores and discount department stores. Some are self-employed, running their own businesses instead of working for others.

Pharmacists also work in hospital pharmacies, where they prepare medicines for patients in the hospital's various wards and departments.

Not all pharmacists work in health care. Some work for **pharmaceutical companies** with other scientists, developing and testing new drugs.

Modern pharmacists deal with a wide range of drugs and medicines, manufactured by many huge pharmaceutical companies.

Main responsibilities of a pharmacist

Pharmacists are responsible for the health and well-being of the customers who bring them prescriptions. The prescriptions, which are instructions written by doctors, tell pharmacists which drugs or medications, in exactly what amounts, each person requires.

When a pharmacist receives a prescription, his or her most important responsibilities include:

- validating the prescription, which means checking the information and, if there are any concerns, contacting the doctor who wrote the prescription to resolve any problems
- making up the prescription, precisely as written
- checking the medication to make sure it is the correct amount and dosage
- giving the medication to the customer
- instructing the customer on how to properly use the medication

A pharmacist must be very careful to make sure a patient is given the correct amount of a prescribed drug.

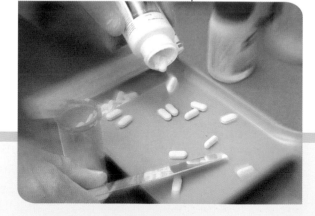

Good Points and Bad Points

"I work in a large pharmacy and help a lot of people. The most satisfying part of the job is offering customers good service."

"At times, the pharmacy is so busy that the process of checking and rechecking the prescriptions for each customer becomes very stressful. With people's health, however, there is no room for error."

The work of hospital pharmacists is similar to retail pharmacists. In hospitals, however, pharmacists work as part of teams, advising medical staff on the best drugs and medicines for individual patients and the correct amounts to prescribe.

Whether they work in hospitals or stores, all pharmacists have a responsibility to make sure that all prescription medicines and drugs are stored safely and do not get into the wrong hands. Pharmacists must keep detailed records, each day, listing all of the prescription drugs in stock and exactly what has been used or sold.

Customers often ask their local pharmacists for information and advice about various drugs and medicines.

Main qualifications of a pharmacist

Scientific knowledge
Pharmacists train for many years. They have to know a great deal about a wide variety of substances and their effects on the human body.

Customer service skills
A pharmacist's customers, who are often worried about their own health or the health of family members, will frequently ask for advice about prescription drugs and nonprescription medicines. Pharmacists must try to be as helpful as possible and must always make sure that customers understand how to take the medications they purchase and are informed about all possible side effects. Some drugs, for example, might cause an upset stomach if they are not taken with food.

A pharmacy's supplies of all prescription drugs must be very carefully monitored.

Responsibility
Every day, pharmacists deal with powerful medicines. They must make sure that they, and all other staff members, follow strict safety guidelines. All pharmacies, whether in stores or hospitals, must be secure at all times to make sure that drugs are not stolen or tampered with.

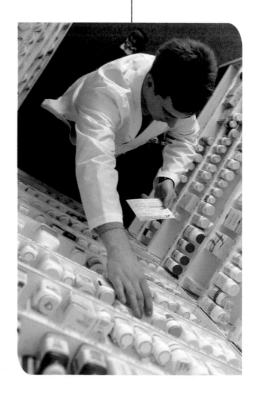

Cautiousness
Even when working quickly and under pressure, pharmacists need to check prescriptions carefully and make sure that the amounts prescribed are correct and that people are not taking products that react against each other.

Knowing how to use computers is an essential skill for pharmacists these days.

fact file

All pharmacists must be licensed in their states of employment. Getting a license requires a degree from an accredited college of pharmacy, followed by 1,500 hours of training as an **intern** in a pharmacy practice and successful completion of a state licensing examination.

Computer skills

Because records of patients and medicines are stored in computers these days, all pharmacists must have good computer skills.

Business skills

To be successful, self-employed pharmacists must be well organized and have many other business skills.

Patsy McGee

Patsy is a licensed pharmacist who works in a hospital.

9:00 a.m. I usually have a number of prescriptions waiting for me when I start work each day. For each prescription, I verify the information, then give it to a technician who processes prescriptions through our computer system. After I prepare the medications, I check them carefully, and send them to nurses, who give them to the patients at the prescribed times, in the prescribed amounts.

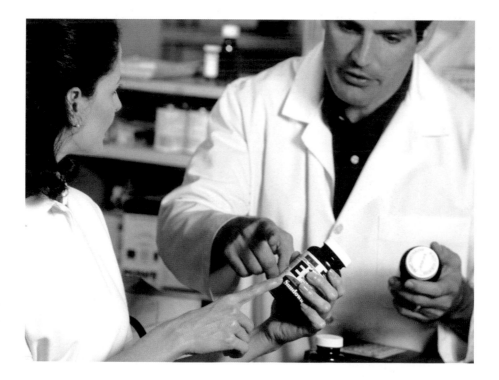

Pharmacists also give patients advice and instructions on medicines, vitamins, and other supplements that do not require prescriptions. Nonprescription medicines and health supplements are commonly referred to as "over the counter" products.

11:30 a.m. I receive a prescription for a newly admitted patient who is taking a drug we don't keep in stock. I contact the patient's doctor to explain the problem, and I suggest an alternative.

12:30 p.m. At lunchtime, I usually eat in the hospital cafeteria with other hospital staff members.

1:00 p.m. Every afternoon, I visit the wards and check patients' drug charts. I am responsible for two wards. I get information from the notes on the charts and speak to doctors, nurses, and even patients, themselves, to help me find ways to improve their drug treatments and medications.

5:00 p.m. My day ends with a patient who is having a difficult time swallowing a high dose of **morphine**. I talk to the patient's doctor and suggest using patches so the drug can be released through the patient's skin.

A pharmacist must carefully check each prescription before filling it.

Glossary

agencies – organizations that represent groups of workers in particular fields and help coordinate employment

agitated – stirred up or jumpy due to troubled feelings or emotional distress

ailments – illnesses, diseases, or other kinds of physical or mental distress

anemia – an ailment in which a person's blood has less than the normal number of red blood cells, causing the person to look pale and feel exhausted

anesthetics – druglike substances used to cause unconsciousness or a loss of feeling in some area of the body

anorexia – short for "anorexia nervosa," which is a serious eating problem that leads a person to starvation due to an intense fear of gaining weight

anxiety – overwhelming worry that often involves both emotional pain and physical symptoms, such as a rapid heartbeat or difficulty breathing

botany – the study of flowers and plants

brain tumors – abnormal growths or swellings on the brain

bulimia – a serious eating problem that involves a psychological need to overeat, usually followed by forced vomiting due to the guilt of overeating

crown – a false tooth that fits over a damaged or decayed tooth

day centers – places that offer supervision and assistance during the day for adults who often have mild physical or mental disabilities and need a safe place to eat meals, socialize, and perform activities

dentures – a complete set of false teeth

depression – a serious psychological state of unhappiness, hopelessness, and fear, usually over a long period of time

diabetes – an illness that results when a person's body cannot control its own blood sugar levels

dietitians – health professionals who are trained to advise people in matters related to foods, eating habits, and meals

disabilities – all types of physical or mental damage that prevent the normal functioning of a person's body or mind

general practitioner – a doctor who serves the general community, treating patients with a wide range of usually common illnesses and injuries

hygiene – the practice of cleanliness for the purpose of maintaining good health

hygienists – licensed health professionals who specialize in oral care, or the health and hygiene of mouths, teeth, and gums

intensive care – a special level of hospital care for patients who are very ill or seriously injured and need medical care and supervision around the clock

intern – an advanced student, in a field such as teaching or medicine, who is actively working in the profession to get practical, supervised training

laboratories – places containing scientific equipment where tests and experiments are carried out

LASIK – the short term for "laser-assisted *in situ keratomileusis*," which is a surgical procedure that uses a laser to reshape the cornea of the eye to improve eyesight and reduce the need for eyeglasses or contact lenses

lenses – pieces of precisely curved glass or plastic that are used to correct eyesight

mood swings – rapid and extreme changes in a person's emotional state

morphine – a strong, addictive drug used to relieve extreme pain

optic nerve – the nerve in the human eye that carries information about what the eye sees to the brain

pharmaceutical companies – large corporations that develop, manufacture, test, and distribute drugs used for medical purposes

phobias – unusual, unexplainable, and illogical fears

private practices – businesses in which professionals are self-employed, which means they work for themselves and personally take all the risks and benefits

psychiatrists – medical doctors who specialize in mental health and the treatment of mental illnesses

scaling – the cleaning process to remove tartar from a tooth's surface

scans – cross-section images of internal organs used to find tumors and other abnormalities that might not show up on normal X rays

social workers – trained professionals who help people with certain kinds of psychological and emotional problems as well as severe economic and social difficulties

specialize – to become an expert in a specific area of professional work or study

sterilizing – thoroughly cleaning to remove germs and bacteria as well as dirt

surgeon – a doctor who specializes in repairing or removing parts of the human body by performing operations

therapists – health care professionals who specialize in the use of, usually, nonmedical methods and procedures for treating physical, mental, emotional, and behavioral problems

vital signs – heart rate, blood pressure, body temperature, and other indicators that a body is alive and well

X rays – photographs taken by passing a stream of radiation through the body to reveal bones and organs

Further Information

This book does not cover all of the jobs that involve working in health care. Many jobs are not described, including physical therapist, hospital administrator, and physician's assistant. This book does, however, give you an idea of what working in health care is like.

Health care professions involve helping people, which can be very satisfying. It is important to remember, however, that the work can be tiring and messy, the hours are often long, and not everyone with health problems recovers, no matter how well the patient is cared for. Health care workers need to be able to deal positively with loss as well as with success.

The way to decide if working in health care is right for you is to find out what the work involves. Read as much as you can about health-related careers and talk to people, especially people you know, who work in health care professions.

When you are in middle school or high school, a teacher or career counselor might be able to help you arrange some work experience in a certain career. For careers working in health care, that experience could mean doing some volunteer work at a hospital, medical center, or nursing home, watching what goes on and how people who work there spend their time.

Books

*Careers without College:
    Home Health Aide*
E. Russell Primm
(Capstone Press, 1998)

*A Day in the Life of
    a Doctor*
Mary Bowman-Kruhm,
(PowerKids Press, 2001)

*Doctors in Action:
    The Orthopedist*
Lee Jacobs
(Blackbirch, 1998)

*Toothworms & Spider
    Juice: An Illustrated
    History of Dentistry*
Loretta Frances Ichord
(Millbrook Press, 2000)

Web Sites

*Jobs for kids who
    like Science*
www.bls.gov/k12/html/
    edu_sci.htm

*Nursing, Psychiatric, and
    Home Health Aides*
www.bls.gov/oco/
    ocos165.htm

*Planning a Career
    in Nursing*
www.ana.org/about/
    careerlt.htm

Useful Addresses

Dentist

American Dental Association
211 East Chicago Avenue
Chicago, IL 60611-2678
Tel: (312) 440-2500
www.ada.org

The American Dental Hygienists'
   Association
444 North Michigan Avenue,
   Suite 3400
Chicago, IL 60611
Tel: (312) 440-8900
www.adha.org

Doctor

American Medical Association
515 N. State Street
Chicago, IL 60610
Tel: (800) 621-8335
www.ama-assn.org

Home Health Care Provider

National Association for Home Care
228 7th Street, SE
Washington, DC 20003
Tel: (202) 547-7424
www.nahc.org

Mental Health Worker

National Mental Health Association
2001 N. Beauregard Street, 12th floor
Alexandria, VA 22311
Tel: (703) 684-7722
www.nmha.org

NAMI (National Alliance for the
   Mentally Ill)
Colonial Place Three
2107 Wilson Boulevard, Suite 300
Arlington, VA 22201-3042
Tel: (800) 950-6264 or (703) 524-7600
www.nami.org

Nurse

American Nurses Association
600 Maryland Avenue, SW
   Suite 100 West
Washington, DC 20024
Tel: (800) 274-4262 or (202) 651-7000
www.ana.org

Alliance for Psychosocial Nursing (APN)
6900 Grove Road
Thorofare, NJ 08086-9447
Tel: (856) 848-1000
www.psychnurse.org

Optometrist

American Optometric Association
243 North Lindbergh Boulevard
St. Louis, MO 63141
Tel: (314) 991-4100
www.aoanet.org

Pharmacist

American Pharmacists Association
2215 Constitution Avenue, NW
Washington, DC 20037-2985
Tel: (202) 628-4410
www.aphanet.org

Index